Internet Marketing For Practitioners

Scott Gallagher

ISBN: 1530611350
ISBN-13: 9781530611355

DEDICATION

This book is dedicated to all the men, women, teens and children who aspire to live the entrepreneurial dream in a democratic environment. I give thanks to the technology era, while we further expose ourselves, we can leverage the Internet era to flourish the dream that the little guy can still make it. I dedicate my work, effort, direction, ideas and passion put forth in my work to and from my mother.

Forewords

This book has come from several years worth of work and education, experience as a business owner and active father. After graduating with a bachelor of Commerce with a specialty in marketing in 2000, I opened my first small business-marketing agency in 2005. With the success of our clients in the courier industry, I became the founder of the first National same day ecommerce delivery company in the United States. It was at this time when I recognized my passion for teaching and founded a firm to teach Internet Marketing to marketers. Now I'm achieving my goal, teaching simple Internet Marketing principals to the local business owner.

Our industry of Internet marketing has become very confusing and cluttered with technology gurus, executives, spammers and newbies. This has made it very difficult for the local business owner to push their business through.

Fortunately great companies like Google were built on something organic. Like the food you eat, organic is good. Word of mouth advertising is the best form of marketing, it's organic, it's natural. While Google is a massive company with dozens of amazing products, their foundation is search. Organic search you can't buy results. Hence Google must give great results, make their 'users' happy, or they won't come back. That's why Google is

Google, they did a great job at providing good organic results.

This is to our benefit. In order to provide good organic results, Google tends to look at good organic factors, like word of mouth advertising. If you're considering a meal at a restaurant and it's busy, chances are they have good food.

The point is, Google's goal to provide results that will make their users happy. If Google is showing busy restaurants that have had other happy customers, then Google's users will continue to remain faithful to Google, and in turn, consume Google's advertising...which is how they make money.

Give them something great for free, and they'll keep coming back.

Internet Marketing is just about good marketing. It's not about understanding and knowing the 200 different factors the Google algorithm looks at, or the most recent algorithm update that affected a bunch of websites.

With my years of experience as a marketer, two decades of B2B sales experience, my education and being a small business owner myself, I've created this book with the intentions to have a step-by-step strategy to help the small business owner achieve the #1 spot on Google.

I assure you, this is not difficult. You do not need a degree, or understand how Google works. This is not about the latest craze on Facebook, nor will you have to be connected to your smartphone, tablet and laptop.

You will have to continue to do what you do best. Service your customers, patients, clients, whatever. Do what you love. This book will not help you if you do not have a sound business with happy customers. This book is about discovering how to leverage everything you already have, and I bet you don't know everything you can leverage.

Praise for Author

DAN THIES
SEO Braintrust

Scott is an Officially Certified Friend of the SEO Braintrust, and an expert in local business marketing. When we want to know what the heck is going on with Google's local search, figure out what some new change, tweak, or offer means... we go to Scott and say, "what's up with that?

CLIFF CALDERWOOD

Upton, MA
www.nelocalmarketing.com

New England
LOCAL MARKETING

Scott's local marketing course gave me the confidence to market myself to local businesses and know the product I was offering was superior to any competitors because of my training. It provided a solid understanding of what to do and what was involved so I knew how much to charge and walk away from bad deals.

EVA JONSHULT

Austin, TX
www.sweepemarketing.com

The program gives you step by step instructions for SEO to get local websites to #1. I now feel confident that I know what I'm doing when it comes to SEO because it works. I like that I can always go back and review a part of the training if I feel I'm missing something.

CARL GATES

Horsham
West Sussex
www.carlgates.com

I like that Scott interacts with his students on a regular basis and says it how it 'is'. It has helped me think of new ways and ideas to implement strategies. Everyone needs to learn somewhere and Scott and the rest of the gang practice what they preach and are down to earth honest guys. So it's saved me time and money searching around falling for so called gurus who try to upsell you the earth wih the latest systems.

I spend my time teaching, speaking, researching and testing Internet Marketing for small businesses.

I have studied sales and marketing for over 20 years, coupled with my marketing education, I begun promoting and developing Internet Marketing Strategies for Local Businesses through search.

Here you'll find comprehensive strategies to ranking your business in the number one spot in the number one search engine, Google.

Enjoy,

Scott P. Gallagher

Table of Contents

Local Search Marketing Industry

The 'Internet Marketing' Industry is being hammered; it's a highly unregulated, fragmented industry with little oversight, far-reaching best practices and simply poor business models. The results have been businesses with little results, agencies and 'experts' with poor communication & execution and simply an industry with a poor image.

Marketing a local business on the Internet seems much more complex than it really is. Let's face it, you'll find the 80/20 rule in many areas of most businesses, whether it's the finance department, operations, sales, marketing or even with human resources. Something I learned early in sales was that 20% of the sales force brought in 80% of the business. Interestingly, the Internet is no different.

80/20 Rule

I find the 80/20 rule all over the place. Imagine if there were 100 different things out there a search engine looks at to evaluate which website it should rank first, second, third and so forth. You'd suspect that changing the top 20 of them would make the greatest impact, if the 80/20 rule applies.

Well if you suspected that I'm going to say, it does apply, drop the suspense, because I am saying that. But it does get interesting.

While Google is a search engine, which is essentially a mathematical computer algorithm with human programmers, it does consider only metrics, numbers….as in factors that can be measured.

So it's natural for our industry to try and understand these things and then try to replicate what we suspect the search engines want. Truth is, this is where 80% of the SEO industry plays.

I don't. Those 20% of the factors I'm talking about can surely be measured. We surely can replicate them and satisfy the needs of the search engine. But the easiest way to do this is with marketing. Real, Old School Business Marketing.

It's just Marketing

The American Marketing Association defines marketing as:

> *Marketing is the activity, set of institutions, and processes for creating, communicating, delivering, and exchanging offerings that have value for customers, clients, partners, and society at large"*

A simple Google search defines marketing as:

> *The action or business of promoting and selling products or services*

At the end of the day, marketing a business requires creating material consumable by your audience and distributed when they may reside.

You hand out your business card at a trade show. You put an ad on the radio in the right time slot. You create a multimedia presentation. You rent bill board space, decal your cars, sign on the front. You get the point.

I'm going to show you how to rank your business number one on Google simply by focusing on simple marketing principals that you've been accustom to for decades, except applying the principal of the Internet.

Changing the Paradigm

Google's mission has provided the opportunity for every type of business to flourish in ways that weren't impossible before.

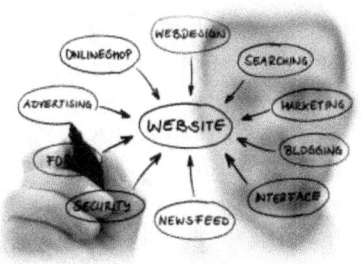

When people want to find something, buy something, research a purchase, they jump on the Internet – at home or on their phone and do a search. If they don't see your business in the results, they won't know you exist; won't buy from you. It's that simple.

Whatever you are paying for newspaper, radio or other such traditional advertising – your dollars will go much further online. However, getting **Qualified Online Traffic** into your business can be very confusing.

→ **Web designers** will say you need a new website.

→ **Search Engine Optimization Experts** will argue that the problem lies in your low ranking.

→ **Copywriters** will say that it's your marketing message.

→ **Social Networking Experts** will say you need to be Tweeting, and Facebooking.

→ **Yellow Pages Reps** will say you *must have* an ad in the Online Yellow Pages.

→ **Branding Experts** will say, yes, you guessed it, the branding and positioning of your company is the problem.

And then there are the larger advertising agencies that take

care of all of the above. They'll say *everything* is the problem.

I wonder. Who is really on your side? Who is looking at the big picture?

Unlike any other type of traditional advertising (newspaper, magazines, radio, tv),…

→ **Internet marketing can be tracked** for results: number of searches, clicks, page views etc. So, you'll know right away whether your online presence is bringing in business.

→ **Search engine rankings are self-evident**. Higher rankings = more traffic coming into your business than lower rankings (your competitors).

→ **Internet marketing can be optimized** over time to ratchet up traffic coming into the business. With analytics installed, it's easy to see where the weak links are and optimize them for ever more traffic and conversion.

There's nothing pie-in-the-sky about marketing online. It's safe, can be tracked and is by far the ***highest return on investment*** compared to any other advertising outlet.

Now, let's dig a little deeper…

The Big Advertising Shift

OFFLINE

➢ Newspapers

➢ Print Yellow Pages

➢ Radio

➢ Cable

ONLINE

➢ Search Engine Marketing

➢ Email Marketing

➢ Social Media Marketing

Consider the following consumer behavior:

➢ "70% of US household now use the Internet as an information source when shopping locally for products and services" (Kelsey Group)

➢ 41% of all business buyers turn to a Search Engine first when looking for a locally based product or service

Got Mobile Internet?

"There are an estimated 4 billion mobile phones worldwide. 130 million web enabled phones just in the U.S. This number is rapidly increasing and will

➢ Product Research and Comparison shopping happens online, but 67% of those purchases happen **offline** *(Accenture)*

➢ 90% of purchases are made within 50 miles of a person's home *(Kelsey)*

Consider the following local search data:

> - 43% of all searches on the Google network included a geographical identifier.
>   - o 86% of those people followed up with a phone call
>   - o 61% of those people ended up making a purchase offline
>
> - 25% of all commercial Internet Searches are conducted by users looking for Local Merchants *(Kelsey)*
>
> - 50% of all Searches are 'local' *(Bing)*
>
> - 84% of U.S. based Internet users performed local searches, or 129 million people, and were looking for a local business

Search Engines drive more traffic to a Website than ALL other mediums combined!

The point is local businesses are transferring their spending from traditional means to an online medium.

A Fresh and Focused Approach

You may have tried some online marketing tactics in the past and failed. You're the norm, not the exception.

Online marketing is easy, just not simple to learn. There is just so much bad information out there.

Incapable people are slamming the industry, and failures are giving the industry a bad name.

Be very careful of those things people tell you that they 'tweaked' a website to rank higher. Here is a document put together by Google that EVERY buyer of online services needs to see.

Visit this URL and I advice your to read this document from Google.

http://bit.ly/What_Google_Says

or scan the following QR code

Here are a few things from Google's site:

- **BE WARY OF SEO FIRMS AND WEB CONSULTANTS OR AGENCIES THAT SEND YOU EMAIL OUT OF THE BLUE.**

- **NO ONE CAN GUARANTEE A #1 RANKING ON GOOGLE**

- **BE CAREFUL IF A COMPANY IS SECRETIVE OR WON'T CLEARLY EXPLAIN WHAT THEY INTEND TO DO**

- **BE SURE TO UNDERSTAND WHERE THE MONEY GOES**

Websites – Your Tool to Convert Clients

Do you remember when people would visit a family doctor if anything was wrong? That doctor was essentially a jack-of-all-trades in the medical field. Their advice was the end all, be all.

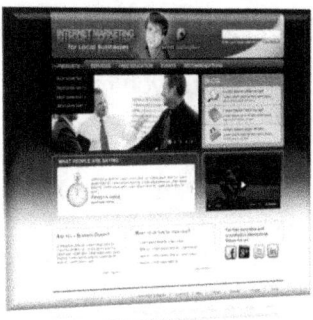

Now medicine has sub-sectors. Doctors specialize into neurology and other medical fields. In fact, there are subspecialties of the neurology specialty.

There is a specialist for everything.

Way, way back in 1995 there was the IT guy. He knew IT, software and websites. He was so smart, everyone looked up to him. Now days I still get called an IT geek, but that is dead wrong.

Just because I work on the Internet, I should know how to fix the computer?

Sure, I probably know more than most, but don't call me to fix your computer.

YOU WOULDN'T HIRE A CARPENTER TO SELL YOUR HOUSE. DON'T HIRE A WEB DEVELOPER TO MARKET YOUR WEBSITE.

Make sure you understand that marketing a website is completely different from creating a website.

Imagine a site that doesn't speak to the right audience. What would this do to YOUR business?

Imagine if you could just double the call-to-action rates (call you, email you, fill out a form, etc.) on the site with a small investment. How would your business be different doubling the number of calls?

Simple keyword research will demonstrate that people are looking for a product or service – in your area - right now!

Once you have that traffic streaming to your site, you must maximize the conversion and the website is a critical component.

A WEBSITE SHOULD TOUCH FIVE SEPARATE HANDS:

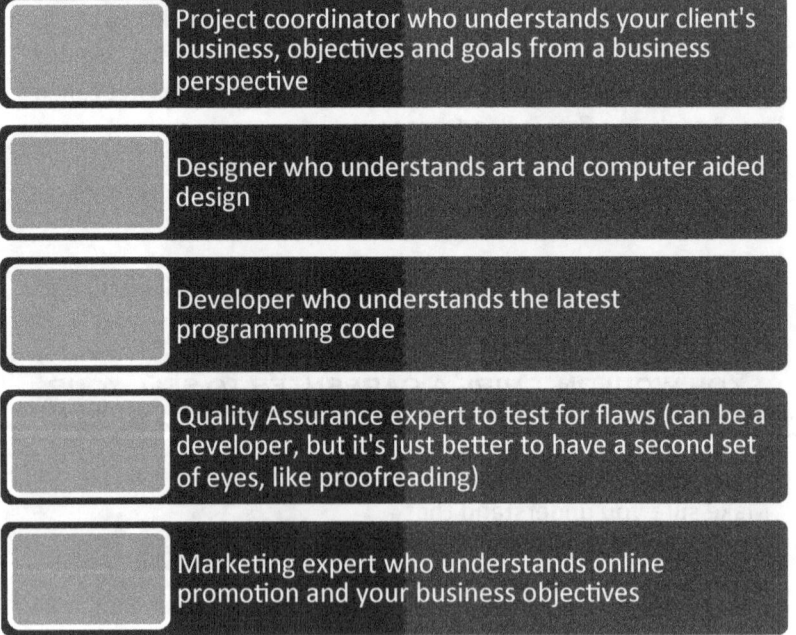

Project coordinator who understands your client's business, objectives and goals from a business perspective

Designer who understands art and computer aided design

Developer who understands the latest programming code

Quality Assurance expert to test for flaws (can be a developer, but it's just better to have a second set of eyes, like proofreading)

Marketing expert who understands online promotion and your business objectives

White and Black Hat Online Marketing

In the days of old western movies, the good guys wore the white hats and the bad guys wore the black hats.

This is no different in our current world of online marketing.

We have all heard of spam email. Something that is spam comes from someone who is black hat.

Another example of black hat online marketing is using techniques that are disapproved of by the search engines in order to increase your rankings.

Basically, you're trying to fool the search engines.

White hat is where we play

This is the more difficult route to win online in the short-term; however, it is the most sustainable and ultimately conforms to the guidelines set forth by the online community who represent paying customers to any local business.

Don't try and fool the search engines

Since it all comes down to the search engines, you must understand their role.

A search engine's job is to provide the most relevant results to a web surfer for the search query requested. Period.

Back in 1998 when Google was founded they gained tremendous market share for one main reason.

It wasn't their marketing. It was their algorithm

An algorithm is a mathematical function (equation) the search engines use to determine the ranking of a webpage (notice I said webpage, not website!). Google's algorithm is so good that by 2002 both MSN (now Bing) and Yahoo! had followed Google's style of ranking.

Since the search engines' role is to provide relevant results, the way they determine if a webpage is relevant is very important.

But their algorithm is constantly changing, thereby making it very difficult to completely understand what is needed to rank in the top spots.

The Local Internet Marketing Fundamentals

I'm going to cover the three major pillars of local search, which are Listings, Citations and Reviews

Listings

First we'll look into listings. We are going to take a look at the types and locations of results in the triggers that indicate to a search engine that it is a local search. We're also going to consider the three major search engines that are currently players in the local game.

Citation and Links

Some people say citations are the new link. If you recall from marketing principles, a website or businesses' transparency and exposure on the Internet from high authority sources is what will get that business exposed in the search engines. In order to increase the businesses trust, citations from trusted websites are required.

Citations are merely Web references of the company in question. When referencing a company online, there are certain pieces of information that are important to reference such as the company name, it's address and its unique local phone number. We call this NAP, N . A . P . for name, address, and phone number

Reviews and Check-Ins

 Reviews are a very important part of the local business marketing strategy. In fact, I believe the reviews are likely the single most important factor in marketing a business online. Not for just for ranking, but overall marketing initiatives.

There are so many reasons why reviews play such a significant role in marketing the local business online from possibly influencing the search results to dramatically improving or hurting perspectives conversion to the call to action.

Customer reviews are merely the digital form of word of mouth advertising. It has been said for centuries that the best form of marketing any business could ever potentially receive this free word-of-mouth and by employing certain campaigns internally at your business you can drive system reviews to your company.

Reviews are becoming a very important part of establishing different factors within the local business results listings and their respective rankings.

 For example, the concept of social review ranking is not being discussed anywhere where implementing systems to measure and monitor and understand how the search engines are deploying review ranking algorithm systems and how the search engines are building social profiles of online reviewers to determine different review patterns.

This is one of those topics that can be very simple and become very complex. Because of the sheer importance of reviews, we have gone to great lengths to understand the system while marketing a business online.

While I believe that the difference between organic search engine optimization and optimizing for the local business results will become closer and closer together, today there are still different strategies.

The biggest difference that will separate the two organic search engine strategies, SEO and Local, is that the process of search engine optimization is still ranking websites and the latter is ranking a business.

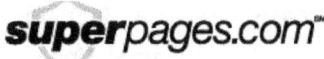

Local Listings

Each of the major search engines have a different philosophy under local ranking, but there is one major common similarity among all three. They started their business ranking websites, now the search engines have the power to rank which businesses the general population chooses to do business with.

With the introduction of integrated results on Google's main search engine results page showed different types of results from the traditional organic listings and PPC. These integrated results included different rich media such as images and videos, included news and social media tweets.

According the Kelsey Group, 43% of ALL searches included a geo-mod on the mainstream search page. Geo-mod is a geographical modifier that dictates to a search engine where to conduct a geographical search. However, this is likely going to decrease as the search engines become smarter about assuming the location and educating users that they do not require a geo-mod with their search to get local results.

Local On-The-Page Factors

As mentioned when I am talking about on the page factors for local business I am not referencing your website and you should follow all the standard principles taught in white hat search engine optimization for organic results. Because we are talking about local businesses here, you should by default have the address of the business on the appropriate pages of that local businesses website. You might have location pages and you might have contact us pages and your name address and phone number should appear on these pages. We call this our NAP, short for Name, Address and Phone number. More on that later.

So we're talking about the places page in the local business center of a search engine.

Because the places page is typically created before it is attached to the businesses Google account, a local business must claim that listing as their own and verify that they in fact are the owner of that listing.

In the local on the page factors video I am going to be covering several of the factors that need to be considered when claiming, creating or completing a business listing profile page within one of the search engines listings.

Types and Location of Results

Since location is an extremely important part of the local business, location is a main factor in determining these results and there are many triggers such as a geo-mod or physical GPS location of the searcher to determine the local results. We need to further understand the triggers.

The location of the local business results varies . Since the introduction into mainstream results in 2009 we have seen a tremendous amount of variation on the placement of the local business results for both when a geo-mod is used and when a geo-mod is not used. This has made it a very difficult process to pinpoint and accurately teach exactly what factors are involved in the placement of the local business results.

It is clear however that the local business results when triggered always are placed above the fold and almost always show at the very top when a geo-mod is used. When considering the blended organic results this is not always true. As of December 2011 all three major search engines are still providing a variety of results for similar searches with different geo-mods. Let's take a look.

We are seeing three types of results in all three of these searches.

1. Organic
2. Local – Blended (Blended Local / Organic)
3. Local – Pack (Local Pack)

This is still a major problem for all search engines today. The problem becomes that a search engine is a single tool for practically an infinite number of different types of people. Each individual might have a different objective when trying to search in a single platform.

Understanding individual needs helps the search engine personalize results. In order to maximize the businesses exposure, a combination of a well-designed website and stable online profiles is required in order to achieve success online.

Local Search Results Triggers

With the introduction of integrated results on Google's main SERP, Google was showing different types of results from the traditional organic listings and PPC. These integrated results included different rich media such as images and videos, included news and social media tweets.

Let me demonstrate. Okay, a search for Barack Obama gives us 3 recent News stories, Obama's website, Wikipedia, live twitter feed, youtube videos, 3 sponsored links, social media profiles, listing of books, images, related searches and now links to more on each of these subjects.

A search for McDonalds gives us the main link, corporate head office, nutritional facts, a Wikipedia entry, news results and a MAP with the three closes locations.

So the question is how does Google know where I'm located to give me locations of McDonald's close to me?

Let's try another search and include a term to tell Google to find me and McDonald's close to my physical location. Try [McDonalds in Algonquin].

Now we get very different results. The map result is right at the top and we only have two results this time in the map. The third result is a directory for the county. The following result is the head office company that runs the local McDonald's and then it is McDonald's corporate office. Next we find some directory information that includes some review information as well as some obscure result for the McDonald's campus in Oak Brook since McDonald's head office is just down the street from us.

The point that we're trying to identify here is that there are certain triggers that tell Google what type of results to display. Whether it be the news or images the Google local map is just another factor in Google's integrated results home page

Well since Google places is a place for businesses to list themselves whether they have a website or not on the Internet, Google basically has to decide if the search phrase being used is looking for a business close to a specific location. This means that there are certain search phrases that trigger the results with a map and other search phrases that don't.

A geo-mod can be any term that signifies a geographical location, such as a city, town, village, airport code, zip code, postal code, local jargon, state, country, county among many other terms. Obviously when a searcher uses a geo-mod it is fairly clear cut that a searcher is looking for local information and enhance like Google gave me the locations of McDonald's first when I included a geo-mod.

But the question becomes what triggers the local business results to come up when we do not include a geo-mod and how does the search engine know where I'm located.

Obviously, when I'm searching from a smart phone most users have their location on and therefore a search engine knows exactly where I'm located. This becomes a little bit more of a challenge with a PC. Your location is typically based on the IP address of your Internet service provider and this poses to be a big problem for a lot of Internet users, such as AOL users because they are always located in California, according to Google and their IP address.

These methods to fine location include IP address, GPS location, cellular triangulation and user input.

The bottom line is that a geo-mod will almost always trigger the local business results and Google is consistently tweaking their algorithm along with personalized search to make their best attempts at trying to determine if that individual searcher is looking for information that has to do with a local establishment.

I also want to point out that many experts claim attaching a website to your places pages helps your rankings on the local business results. I will challenge that claim for the present with many different scenarios, however I am predicting that this in fact will be a factor in the future, it only makes sense.

Local Search Engines

It all depends on whom you are talking to but there is a variety of different local search engines out there. Some people argue that a local yellow page website is a local search engine. A local social network can be considered in the local search umbrella. Let's clarify.

Essentially, we are dealing with data providers, search engines, review sites, local directories and local social networks. Refer to the document titled Client_Inventoy_Assets.xlsx for a complete list of these sites.

Here is a list of local search engines.

- Google places
- Yahoo Local
- Ask City
- Bing Local
- Local.com

- AOL Local
- Citysearch

Between Google, Yahoo and Microsoft, they hold over 90% of the market and therefore these are the three we are going to be looking at today.

Local Search Engines & Popular Local Search Listings

Getting a business listed is easy, all you have to do is decide where you want to begin. Just navigate to http://bit.ly/lmsplaces to find links on how to claim listings for each of the three major search engines.

Claiming and Correcting Listings

Unfortunately, not all business owners have come to the realization that they do not have to passively let these interactive web pages exist. There are those business owners that have caught on quickly if they claim and update their local business listing, they can use this as a local marketing tool.

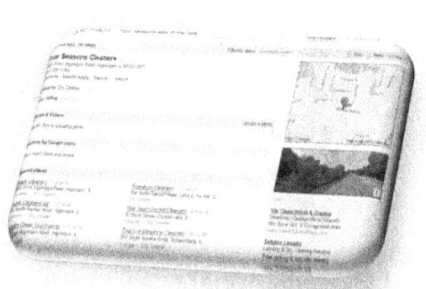

In order to make these interactive pages a benefit for a local business, the first step is to claim the listing before you can update the listing with the business marketing material. There are typically four methods being employed to verify the authenticity of the claimant

1. E-Mail
2. Postcard in the mail with a Pin code

3. Phone call to your business phone number with a pin code
4. Manual verification

Depending upon the local listing website, some allow you all of these options while others begin charging a fee for enhanced listing. Recently we have seen the search engines restricting how easy it is to claim a particular listing. In fact, we are seeing the majority of listings only able to be verified via a phone call or snail mail, such is the case with Google, unless there is an abundance of existing trust for that business.

The claiming process is important because if say a competitor gets access to the local business listing they can detract customers to a different location by phone or by website address. In addition, the damage that can be done might include incorrect information on photos, videos, coupons, and much more. Because consumers are using the local business listings to locate a business, product or service in their area, by phone or website, the security around local business listings has to be high priority for any local listing website. If you are having problems in this area, links to help are found at http://bit.ly/lmsplaces.

Ranking Methodology

Our ranking methodology is very simple.

Qualified traffic + Conversion = Sales.

The goal of marketing a business on the Internet is to provide your clearly defined target audience with a high impact, high value interactive experience.

While this is simple, it is not easy. We do this by creating effective transparency for the business and exposing the business in the appropriate areas of the Internet that their target audience is hanging out.

Therefore, whether we consider search engine optimization, paid advertising, e-mail marketing or social media marketing, the goal essentially remains the same and the goal's answer lies in your marketing principles. Online Marketing efforts should provide your target audience with a high impact, high value experience while they're spending their time online considering the business in question.

This is fairly simple to accomplish, just not easy. We accomplish this goal by providing high-quality effective transparency and exposure of the business online. For example, having a testimonial video and uploading to YouTube and embedding that video into your blog and sending people from your e-mail list to your blog is creating that exposure a business requires. The greater the exposure, the greater the quality, the greater authority a search engine will assign to that business and in turn provide greater exposure on their search engine.

We focus 80% of our efforts on 20% of the activities that yield 80% of the results.

It is nearly impossible for anybody to know all the factors that are involved in ranking. We can only determine these factors are trial and error and testing and of course learning from others. The bottom line is that all the search engines want to see value added to the end-user.

Local on-the-Page Factors for the Website

At first I'm going to talk about the local on the page factors that are relevant for the business website itself. You must not forget about those other organic SEO factors and they must all be properly implemented in addition to some of these am going to discuss right now.

These factors are exclusive to a website for a local business. First let's take a look at location pages. A local business might have several different locations in a specific geographical area. This geographical area might be regional with several states or just within a specific province or state, country or even within a city or suburb. Here were talking about locations that are only relevant for the audience that the business is trying to attract, a warehouse that is never mentioned in typical marketing material does not apply here.

Location pages should be well-defined location pages and have the appropriate geo-mod keywords in the content. This means writing content that is relevant, informative and entertaining for potential customers for the business website. You can further connect with the audience by creating content that discusses the geographical location and local jargon of the area.

This leads me to Geo content. The entire website should have content that is focused around the geographical location as discussed in the organic search results section this information should appropriately fit in to key information such as the title tag, each one and H2 tags, and the anchor text for internal linking within the website.

The entire theme should have Geo intent. When considering topics such as your community, you can create communal of fact by having a common interest of a certain geographical location. Your web 2.0 properties on the website are going to focus on an audience within your service area.

All of your audience messaging on the website is focused around all of the common interests of the audience or potential customers you are trying to reach. Within that geographical area there are many common interests that can be discussed and provided to your audience to interact with. Think of local events, local organizations or businesses, history or local industry.

All of your images should be properly tagged for location and include the geographical location in the Alton information of the title tag for the image.

Your internal linking structure doesn't change too much except for the addition of location pages. All of your products and services pages should have links with the appropriate anchor text linking to all of your location pages. All of your location pages should have links going to all of your service pages with the appropriate anchor text and the geo-mod located around or within the links.

A Review can contain a several different properties which you can label in the HTML code using microdata, microformats, or RDFa markups. Google recognizes the following Review properties, derived from the hReview microformat. This is when you get a testimonial from a customer and you want to display it on your webpage. In Google Webmaster tools search for review data to get specific coding requirements.

Profile Listings & Best Practices

If you visit a site, visit www.getlisted.org, this has a simple little tool in its collecting all which listings on which search engine is claimed and provide links to go ahead and claim the listings.

It is important that your profile is completed 100% or as close to it as possible. When filling out information for any of the fields, your information should be unique and very focused on the customer. Your description should use the entire available space to properly describe the business is in your unique competitive advantage. Remember, always talk about benefits and not features. Remember that search engines read content and tie it to your keywords. Keywords are typically words or phrases that are driven by consumer market demand and in turn, by using the greatest number of searched keywords and placing that in your description, you are merely providing great content to the end-user where a majority of users would use those keywords.

There is the debate on addresses, whether they should be shown or not. One thing that we have found to be true is that non-physical locations, such as a PO box or UPS store box, is a challenging listing to rank. Google doesn't want to rank asset-less companies. Google wants to rank locals and you must have a physical address to properly compete.

In addition to this we suggest this is the time to establish your NAP. This is your name, address, phone number and you should always appear in the exact same format regardless of the online property.

Just like the discussion of photos, videos are merely a different medium to just to view content in the search engines are favoring listings that utilize videos. This is a great opportunity to upload testimonial videos or a walk-through video.

The categories section is one of those sections. Make sure that you use all five of your categories and that you have claimed your category with Google's suggested results first, and any remaining claims to input a custom category which is your number one or top keywords.

Testimonials and reviews are something as you should know are very important.

There are couple of points that I want to remind you of on your places page that are very important to have filled out properly. If it is filled out properly you will vastly increase your chances of getting ranked.

A new section found in Google places that was recently announced as service areas and since its introduction on 4/20/2010, the service area feature does not seem to be working in less there are relevant off the page factors that are present. It is highly suggested to not over estimate your service area and provide Google with accurate data.

Your description section is a section for you to maximize your content. Remember the Google is a huge fan of content and this is an area that all of your services should be covered along with all of your locations and if possible surrounding suburbs.

Avoid These on your Profile Pages

Now moving forward there are six points I want to bring up is highly relevant to avoid using in your local listings.

Stay away from using 800 phone numbers, or as previously mentioned PO boxes or UPS boxes.

Since Google's guidelines indicate that each business can only have one places page per location, and Google is attempting to localize everything, having one main phone number on multiple pages is a big no-no, at least at this time.

If you go to LMS Places, http://bit.ly/LMSplaces , we have compiled a list of links that you can reference for local.

Having different phone numbers on different pages of your website, or different locations through the Internet such as yelp and Google, can also have a negative effect on the Google listing. Sometimes people use different phone numbers for telephone tracking purposes. I generally recommend against this and a local business should never, use more than one phone number per location that is publicly displayed. Forget about the benefit of call tracking analytics for a moment, having multiple phone numbers for one single location from a user standpoint and a memorability standpoint can have a negative effect on the user experience. I'm talking about customer service. It is not good for the end-user . Stay away from this.

And worthy of a mention, albeit violating Google's T&C's, having multiple pages for one single business in one single location will definitely hurt the rankings of all the listings.

Citations and Links

Now that we are reminded that marketing a business on the Internet follows traditional marketing principles, we know from organic search engine optimization that links are very important for ranking and now I am telling you that citations from highly relevant sources are also important. So I guess the question becomes what is the difference between a citation and a link. Let's take a look.

Citations are merely Web references of the company in question. When referencing a company online, there are certain pieces of information that are important to reference such as the company name, it's address and its unique local phone number. We learned this was a N .A .P. for name, address, and phone number.

On occasion, search engines and these data providers collect information from public sources and while it's not as important to ensure that these public sources are accurate, is worthy noting that when dealing with these other sources that you provide them with identical NAP information. For example, when a business requires a business phone number from the local telephone provider, typically they automatically receive insert into their Yellow Pages and upsell ad space. The information provided to the telephone provider should be exactly the same as you would in your Google places account. This is a source of information for Google that they trust.

Local Citation Sources

Data Providers

Following is a list of data providers that search engines pull information from, because as we've discussed Google Places is merely data aggregator. While there are other data providers evidence has clearly indicated that these are the top data providers that Google pulls is information from in these following seven data providers you should check and ensure that the formatting of your NAP is identical from provider to provider.

Major Search Engines

- Google Places
- Yahoo Local
- Bing Local
- Facebook Places

Major Data Providers

- YellowPages.com
- UniversalBusinessListing
- Acxiom
- infoUSA
- localize
- superpages.com
- Yelp
- InsiderPages

Secondary Data Providers & Portals
- Best of the Web Local
- Amazon.com
- Hotfrog
- OpenList
- Dexknows
- Merchant Circle
- InsiderPages
- Discoverourtown.com
- Angies' List
- Judy's Book
- Local.com
- Geo Directories
- Theme Directories
- AOL Local Search
- GetFave.com
- Addresses.com
- GenieKnows.com
- Edmunds.com
- LocalMatters
- UrbanSpoon.com

Public Sources

On occasion, search engines and these data providers collect information from public sources and while it's not as important to ensure that these public sources are accurate, it's worth noting that when dealing with these other sources that you provide them with identical NAP information.

These other sources may include company annual reports, SEC information, federal state and city governments, various business magazines, newspapers and local publications, and Postal Service information.

Of course these public sources are typically for larger firms. As an internal rule of thumb, when a client provides us with over $1000 per month in revenue, we will look at public sources.

- Annual Reports
    - depending on the state, once a business reaches certain revenue mark, or if the business is public, annual reports are published. This is good content to get exposed and perhaps the company blog or a partner's blog. The annual report should be available for download in PDF format and the business NAP should remain consistent.
- SEC Information
    - The mission of the U.S. Securities and Exchange Commission is to protect investors, maintain fair, orderly, and efficient markets, and facilitate capital formation. Located at www.sec.gov is a website to acquire information about a business. Confirm listings here and NAP.
- Federal, State and City Governments
    - When registering your company, you must have it registered with the state, feds and your local business directories. Confirm your NAP in all of these sources.
- Business Magazines
    - Industry and theme magazines are always looking for theme related high quality content. These are sources you can create positive content to help your online exposure.
- Local Newspapers & Local Publications

- o In the next video, we're going to uncover how to find and look for local newspapers and publications to get your content published in.
- Postal Service Information
  - o Ensure the post office is using the same NAP that you have established.

Citations Acquisition Strategies

Local search engines

The search engines crawl each other to find citations that will validate or correct the business information in their own database. Additionally, some engines and data share information with each other typically through a data leasing arrangement or syndication.

For example, you'll frequently see a business's Yahoo Local profile show up in the 'Web Pages' tab of its Google Places Listing. There are other second-tier portals that show up frequently as well, such as dexknows.com and Yelp.com

Local blogs

Local blogs are a great place to get a business listed. These vary by geography, but if you simply perform a search on your favorite engine for "[geomod] blog," you'll see good candidates. Please reference the organic search engine optimization videos on more methods to use the search engines to find theme or local blogs. You can also just use your GeoMod for a standard search in Google and choose the 'blogs' option on the left. Play with this a little, and note the blogs that show up on the top, and stay on the top of the listings when changing the date range. For example, if you search for 'all time' and switch to only the last week and find the same blog, chances are this a highly indexed, popular blog.

The blogs that show up for these kinds of searches are generally very well-indexed by the search engines, and highly associated with a particular neighborhood, city, or region. Businesses that are mentioned or linked on these blogs are viewed as trusted, relevant results in the Local search engines.

Locally-focused directories

Like Local blogs, Local directories are well-indexed by the search engines and are highly associated with a particular city or region. Directories which are edited by a human are much better than those which are built around an algorithm where anyone can enter information. Human-edited directories are less susceptible to spam, and are therefore more trusted by the search engines. Best of the Web's Regional Directory and Yahoo's Regional Directory are two human edited trusted sources. You can perform searches for things like "[geomod] directory" to find good prospects for these kinds of citations.

Theme Based Sites

There are many different ways to acquire authority based theme related exposure on a variety of different sites. For example, most industries have niche-based or industry associations. These associations have opportunities for memberships, typically have online social sites or forums and many have different social media feeds. Participating in these conversations will provide your business with exposure. If you ever get written about, or be one of the faces in the crowd, these theme related authority sites may publish something in your regards. This obviously ties into PR campaigns as previously discussed when putting together a full execution strategy. Do a search for [THEME Social] or [THEME Forum], such as [dentist forum].

Theme Related Citations

When discussing theme related pages, the same principles and strategies taught in Organic Search Engine optimization for theme related directories and data providers will absolutely apply in this case. A search engine is merely referencing the citation rather than a link if you had the opportunity to acquire that link.

Theme related directory for a particular dentist as an example would be a website www.findadentist.com. Sometimes these sites require paid inclusion and this should never be confused with paid money for a link, because you are paying for inclusion into the directory and may or may not get a link.

And finally this leads into theme related authority exposure. There are many different ways to acquire authority based theme related exposure on a variety of different sites. For example, most industries have niche-based or industry associations. These associations have opportunities for memberships, typically have online social sites or forums and many have different social media feeds. Participating in these conversations will provide your business with exposure. If you ever get written about, or be one of the faces in the crowd, these theme related authority sites may publish something in your regards. This obviously ties into PR campaigns as previously discussed when putting together a full execution strategy.

Blogs and Directories

If a website, blog or directory is not focused on a particular geographical region and if that website is focused on topics and keywords related to the audience in question, it is likely a theme related site. For example, take the same day delivery business. There is a social site on the NING network called 'Couriers of the World". The dental industry has Facebook groups, forums and online discussions. the membership directory of your trade organization, or a blog that is popular among readers in your industry will likely be crawled by the Local search engines for citations. Searches like "[geomod] directory" or even "[theme keyword] directory" will give you some ideas of the kinds of sites on which to get listed. Try [theme blog] as well. Reference the organic SEO section for more search phrases.

Social Media

Social media marketing is the art of using different types of media for social interaction, using highly accessible and scalable communication techniques. Social media is the use of web-based and mobile technologies to turn communication into an interactive dialogue.

Essentially, the greater reach with influencers with your content, the greater trust and authority is assigned to that citation source.

Take for example any local greasy spoon restaurant. Guy Fieri is the host to diners, drive-ins and dives, food network's unique television show with a crazy dude the sunglasses and a spiked white hair. What if he came by this local greasy spoon and provided a positive review, either tweeted about it or left a comment on Facebook. One would think as a micro-celebrity that review should have a greater impact than other reviews because he is a well-known food connoisseur and hosts his own food television show. Search engines are looking at many factors to evaluate social profiles in determining relevance and authority for reviews and citations. Therefore some additional factors that should be added to this list could be a user's frequency and geographical footprint pattern to determine the validity of that review or citation.

Thus, using social media as a form of marketing has taken on whole new challenges. It is most effective if marketing efforts

through social media revolve around the genuine building of authority. Someone performing internet marketing for a company must honestly convince people of their genuine intentions, knowledge, and expertise in a specific area or industry through providing valuable and accurate information on an ongoing basis.

There are many ways authority can be created and influence can be accomplished such as: participation in Wikipedia which actually verifies user-generated content and information more than most people may realize. Try providing valuable content through social networks on platforms such as Facebook and Twitter. When you create an article for SEO, tweet it. When a new blog post is created, post a link on Facebook.

Your goal is get the information shared on Facebook, Linkedin or Twitter. If a friend or follower shares your information, each share is a citation. The more shares, the busier the restaurant looks to Google and therefore it'll assign trust towards the business in question.

As a result of social media and the direct or indirect influence of social media marketers consumers are more likely to make buying decisions based on what they read and see in platforms we call "social" but only if presented by someone they have come to trust. That is why a carefully designed social media strategy has become an integral part of any internet marketing plan. This influences both conversion and driving traffic.

Many restaurants have gained success by engaging into this game with their audience and assigning discounts or online only deals.

Consider this. A coupon in a newspaper. As a marketer it's not about reducing the profit but a coupon is meant to increase the volume. What is really messed is the value in the brand of that coupon. I would never keep an advertisement for business but if it's good to get me a free soda next time I get a pizza I will keep that paper indefinitely in my drawer. Every time I open a drawer I see their brand. For this reason we have to rethink the coupon and social media.

As an example, by offering rewards for those that have gained mayorship from foursquare or yelp is a way to encourage repeat business and provide a perception of a certain culture. You can make this fun and in turn you have whole bunch of prospects and customers that are regurgitating and sharing all of your information on their favorite social networks.

Consider creating some viral content. An insurance company might want to discuss the last five years of the rising levels of the local river and their thoughts and implications for what could happen to the town if nothing is done. Maybe this video would be an exaggeration but they could talk about certain buildings that are wiped out. This would create fear in our community and awareness towards this rising river. The author, a local insurance company, would then in turn increase their exposure whether people agree with them or not. This exposure is recognized by the search engines.

One of my clients, a taxi service in Chicago, is including their QR code in the back seat of their taxi. They encourage their customers to scan this code with their smart phone and share their experience in this Online. People are uploading pictures of themselves, leaving reviews and rating an army of links back to my client site. We are not getting the citations or links ourselves, but we are using the power of social media to generate this exposure.

In the past, we have created new Wikipedia pages and send the content sources to authorities in the industry that we know would appreciate it. They in turn share this new valuable information with their friends and followers and give credit to the author, the business in question. Yet another way to generate citations from users

as you can see I can simply just go on and on with a variety of different strategies for social media to acquire links and citations. You must really understand your audience and dig deep to uncover new ways for your audience to enjoy engaging in a conversation related around your business. Once you've discovered this, identifying and implementing a certain strategy for your client or your business is the easy part.

Local PR

It is not that difficult to devise a PR strategy with local newspapers and publications to run content that sites the business in question both in the off-line in the online world and this is a very high authority citation for any local business.

For example, finding and joining local networking groups is not that difficult to get business citation as a member of one of these websites and having the search engines index this information and assign authority and credibility to the business in question.

Joint Ventures

One often overlooked opportunity for local businesses in the online world is to identify joint ventures with other businesses that serve similar audience. For example chiropractor's, massage therapists and dentists could all very easily share their patient database with one another. By identifying local theme related businesses that you can create partnerships with and joint ventures with, having other local businesses cite your

business on their website and their pages is relatively easy to accomplish.

In the case of your Internet marketing agency, a credit card processing firm as an example of an excellent JV. We are both going after the same audience and there was nothing, both direct and indirect, that would be perceived as competition.

Identifying volunteer and donation opportunities through local and theme charities is an excellent opportunity to give a little bit to the community and in turn get referenced online.

Again, this comes down to your audience profiles. By understanding the audience in question, and where they are hanging out on the Internet, will give us great insight into understanding which sites we may want to work with and create a potential partnership with.

Completive Analysis

In marketing principles, competitive research is an extremely important stage in the marketing planning process. The more we can understand about the rights and wrongs of the direct and indirect competition, the better we can position ourselves to market our business or our clients.

Therefore, we are going to take a look at the citations acquired by the competition.

First, let's take a look at what Google might see on our competition. Refer to your competitive research list, which is taught in the Marketing Principals section. You will need your competitive research completed and your strategy map for this exercise.

Do a search for your number one keyword and take a look at the results. Identify who you're top organic and local competitors are and document them on your competitive analysis excel file, including their full NAP and any NAP variations. Then do a Google search for each of their NAPs and variations of their NAP, such as address, business name and DBAs. Scout the top three pages for relevant sources!

In your competitive research file that I hope you have for every one of your clients, list the URL of all your main competitors. Visit each one of those sites and make a determination of whether or not this is a citation that you can acquire. Once you accomplish this step set strategies in motion to contact these sites to acquire the citation. Some of these sites will be different portals, review sites, local and theme blogs and some will not fit into any of these categories. These are citations that you need not acquire.

Local Directories, Publications, Networking Groups

By joining the Chamber of Commerce or different local networking groups is not that difficult to get business citation as a member of one of these websites and having the search engines index this information and assign authority and credibility to the business in question.

I suggest taking that businesses chamber logo and attaching it to the businesses website with a single one-way link to identify from a user value perspective at that local business participates in local networking groups and supports the community.

I joined my chamber of commerce for $20 per month. This is a no-brainer to me for any business to get listed and get a highly trusted citation.

I started a NING social platform for my niche. What about Facebook groups centered on your community? What about parenting forums if your client is a local restaurant?

Think about the business and reference your audience profile sheet. When considering the audience character traits, perhaps dental patients in Vancouver, Canada, consider what's important to them.

Ok, so this dentist we're assuming has positioned themselves around preventative maintenance, rather than say cosmetics, such as teeth whitening. Their patients are those who make an effort to get their teeth cleaned, what to do the work to keep them white and healthy. Being in Vancouver, they're all health nuts, try and find a greasy spoon and it's hard. It's all about salads and weed, odd place.

What do stoned health nuts do online? Well, first I'd start by following some of these people. Twitter search makes this easy to find followers.

Then I'd follow the links they are all talking about. I'd start to collect all these location sites and document them over time. After a few weeks of this system in place, I'll have a great idea of where these people frequent. Everyone on the social sites likes to share information. This information is valuable when trying to understand where our target audience is hanging out.

Non-Conventional Citation Ideas
1. Start Hosting Parties and Events
2. Get a Redbox or ATM at your business
3. Free Wi-Fi
4. Sponsor local events like festivals or charity events
5. Check in deals with Foursquare, Google+, Groupon or Facebook
6. Install a weather monitoring station
7. Add a cellular antenna to your property.
8. Install a Webcam.

Customer Reviews

Considering reviews, we're going to be looking at the benefits of reviews, quantity versus quality, establishing profile Authority and social and review ranking, review filters, review creation, review acquisition strategies and patterns, Rich snippets, review coding and finally an overview of review sites their impact industry perception.

What is a Review?

A review is a personal evaluation of a movie, publication, game, music , book; a piece of hardware like a car, home appliance, or computer; or an event, such as a live music concert, a play, and finally we're here to talk about reviews for businesses, such as Restaurants, dry cleaners, apartment management companies, mechanics, doctors, day spas, limousine services, law firms, and other brick and mortar businesses who lose and gain customers daily based on their past and current customers' opinions.

There are 1000s of local business review sites and directories, but as a business owner, you should first pay attention to the truly important ones already showing up in Google, Yahoo!, and Bing for your keywords. You can list your business on the sites I'm going to talk about later where past and current customers can review for free, although some have paid versions in order to "expand your page" like MerchantCircle and CitySearch, it's not always necessary because they will take reviews all day (more content for them).

Review Benefits

There are many reasons that benefit a local business in terms of reviews. While considering online marketing principles, reviews accomplish three things. Ranking, conversion, and service area. There are many misconceptions about how reviews influence ranking, many don't consider the importance of conversion and finally reviews solve a very common problem among many types of businesses.

Directly from one of Google's own pages when discussing complex code for micro data formatting to convey ratings they have the following text "This section describes how you can mark up your rating information to use images (for example, an image of four stars) to convey ranking information. "

This is yet the only public information from Google that explicitly says reviews influence rank, but this is enough proof for me.

Getting customer reviews is an important step in improving your rankings in the Google Local Business Results. Ask for a review anytime someone compliments your services. Implementing a customer review policy in your company could dramatically improve your rankings.

Ranking

There are several factors that can be measured for particular review by a search engine. For example, quantity of reviews, quality of reviews, review acquisition, location or review, review acquisition patterns among sources, data of sources and of course source politics. We are going to be taking a look at all of these factors and what influence they might have on your ranking.

Conversion

When a prospect lands on a particular places page, we already know that reviews are a high influence towards the consumer's perception of the business. We're going to be considering why only a small number reviews are shown and discussed the social review ranking within these places profiles and how each of these reviews influences the consumers conversion towards a call to action on that business.

We're going to be considering which review sites have high influence within Google places and how to influence the activity in a positive manner for each of those sites. By driving a high quality review system into a local business insurers that properties like Google places only shows reviews that provide the highest conversion to a call to action. While some businesses are focusing on Internet marketing efforts of driving traffic, few go to the length of improving their conversion ratio and therefore there is a massive opportunity to drive a call to action for your clients. Make sure you make this an important part of your strategy for your clients to ensure a high quality service provided to them and to help keep your clients for long-term.

Service Area

Most service-based businesses face a significant problem when marketing themselves on the Internet. For a variety of reasons, different businesses in different geographical areas clearly different service areas. Service area is defined by the area in which the business will provide its services or the geographical reach in which customers will travel in order to do business with that company.

Reviews are a very important part of establishing trust towards establishing your service area in the eyes of online websites like Google places. Let's face it, a business' service area essentially is where their customers reside. Whether it's a business that travels to a consumer's home or business or the company that tracks clientele to its storefront, its service area defined by a web of its customers. We know the search engines know exactly location of where these reviews are being left based on GPS, IP address information, cellular triangulation or user input. When users leave reviews that are trusted more than less authoritative reviewers, those particular reviews provide further trust to a search engines on establishing a web of your reviews.

Local Search Review Profiles

Reviewers, Trust and Authority

A reviewer can either be a guest or a registered user, typically on a review site. We already know that reviews can be left on any website, but trust is assigned to that particular website and review. We are going to be taking a look at a list of sites that we  know of high trusted authorities within the major search engines. Within these sites is a community of registered users. When a registered user leaves a review, that user could have a review that offers tremendous value or could be a bogus review from a competitor. Both the search engine and the review sites and an algorithm are in place to rank reviews

Review Profile Usage Patters

The usage patterns of a particular user within a review site can potentially have many factors that are measured. For example, a reviewer might consistently have reviews that are three stars or less, but we know published by yelp that 85% of all reviews across their site and the web of three stars or more. Therefore the user that consistently has lower score reviews, will be assigned less trust for their reviews because they do not follow the norm of the general population.

Another example is the reviewer that has multiple profiles on multiple sites and leaves multiple negative reviews for one business when this goes against their typical review submission pattern. This would raise a red flag for search engine of less trust within that particular review.

There are likely dozens and dozens of scenarios that we can come up with where consumers try and harm a local business in the search engines but because of filters and an algorithm in place, the review sites and search engines are getting much better at being able to sniff out these people. In other words don't fret from a few negative reviews and focus on pushing your happy customers to leave reviews. When I say pushing, I mean giving them the right tools so they can go ahead and say all those nice things that they are to have been saying.

Establish Profile Authority & Social Review Ranking

Establishing profile Authority can be a little bit of a challenge because you are attempting to influence the customers of your client. You need to work with your client to ensure that they are doing everything they can to help influence acquisitions in a positive manner and in turn focusing on those profiles that have high authority.

It is common sense that a search engine's goal is to provide the best user experience for their own users. It makes sense that the best user experience would be to have the most democratic unbiased information for consumers to make decisions about that business. So, this is what the filters and the algorithms are consistently trying to accomplish. As much as we can try and learn everything we can about all of those factors and give the search engines exactly what we think they want, it is obvious to focus on our clients customers rather than the search engines provide the best user experience.

Profile Authority is established by users who have a common typical review pattern. There are certain norms and thresholds that dictate what a common typical review pattern is, but the easiest way to ensure that your customers are reviewers with high authority are reviewers that essentially engage in a community and a natural organic form. The best way to ensure that are reviewers are natural and organic, is for us to provide the education and the tools to leave these reviews on sites that have high influence and to ensure that these reviewers are consistently engaging in their community and reviewing multiple other businesses in their area.

Drive Education to Build Profile Authority

You have many options available to you on how to drive the appropriate education to your customers' customers.

We are going to take a look at a review acquisition strategy. There is a document that is included in The Accelerated Program for Local Online Marketers course and is intended to help educate our customers' on the process to leave reviews. This is an excellent piece to drive education to your customers to encourage them to encourage their customers to continually leave reviews. I will cover this further in another video.

As you might know, e-mail marketing is a critical strategy for local business to market themselves in my opinion. You can drive short education pieces through e-mail marketing to your customers' customers. This will give you an opportunity to potentially earn the right to providing you know marketing as a service.

With all SEO campaigns now, we install a WordPress blog for our clients. This is another great place to continually drive content about reviews to educate our customers community.

Creating and sending content to be published by local networking groups and theme related sites is a great way to drive education and acquire a citation on your client's behalf.

Obviously, social media campaign with links that drive to content sources that add value to the end-user is a strategy that works well when you have qualified followers or friends.

We can discuss different strategies that you can provide education to the end-user about the value of reviews for both of them and their vendor. The point here is that we have to drive this education to the end-users or our system reviews might fail.

Testimonials and Check-Ins

Testimonials, reviews and check ins are channels of communication from the customer to the business. In essence, this is exactly what business is, communication from a business to a customer and vice versa.

You have a lot of choices on how to market your clients online, but I assure you if you focus your efforts on the one item that is most important to every single business then you will get success for your client. In other words, focus on the customer. Pretty simple, huh?

Testimonials are intermediated word-of-mouth marketing, and they do work when credible. In fact they work very well indeed if you work hard to get the right kind of testimonial. They can provide the much-needed social proof that tips a wavering prospect into a paying customer.

A researcher named Mehrabian was particularly interested in how certain listeners received their information about a speaker's general attitude in situations where the facial expression, tone, and words are sending conflicting signals.

The results are impressive.

- 55% from the visual component
- 38% from the auditory component
- 7% from language

This means that the words we choose influence human behavior with only a weight of 7%, our tonality represents 38% and our physiology represents 55%!

If this is true, then I want video testimonials of people saying great things about my company!

Social Check-Ins

Many social networking services, such as Foursquare, Facebook, Yelp and Gowalla allow users to "check in" to a physical place and share their location with their friends.

Users can check in to a specific location by text messaging or by using a mobile app on a smartphone--the application will use the phone's GPS to find the current location.

Many apps have a "Places" button where a user can see a list of nearby places into which the user can check in. If a location is not on the nearby places list, the user can add the location directly from the phone. Once a user has checked in, they have the option of sharing their location with friends in services such as Twitter or Facebook.

Check-in and Location Based Marketing

Check-ins, badges, Mayors, stamps on passports, rewards, and other new concepts from the past are popping up everywhere on the Internet as the latest trend in location based services are applied to marketing purposes. It's a blast from the past, isn't it? This is just a loyalty program. No different than my coffee punch card, but on steroids. Now I get the 8th cup for free, and all my friends know about it. What about flying? I check-in at the counter. If I give them my information, I get rewards with 'air miles' now when I check in. I do something, exchange some value and then get rewarded if we exchange information. Same model here folks, maybe this will tell us something about how these check-ins might work for a business.

Volume and Velocity

But let's slow down for a moment, there is a big difference between some of the old check-ins the new ones. We know that checking out at a supermarket or checking-in in an airplane typically means an exchange in value. They paid someone. Take Foursquare check-ins....the rewards, on the other hand, are offered to individuals that just showed up. I'm not quite sure yet on this. Rewarding someone for showing up makes little sense. Arguably the reward gets them in the door, and they need to be in the door to buy.

The real value of Check-ins should reward more than just physical presence. But shouldn't the real question be is how you get the customer to the door from the beginning.

Local Search Reviews, Rich Snippets and Ratings

Sometimes I have to do something in this business that isn't so much fun. HTML is one of those. Coding in fact is it. Like accounting, I wish I never have to deal with it but you do.

I'm no coder. But I have to have some knowledge of it, at least from a practical standpoint.

Rich Snippets are a fancy way of saying "I want a review to be on my website and I want Google to count it as a review".

Or I frequently hear that people have a hard time getting a great customer to leave a review. I think of one student of mine, another Scott, who struggled with this because, his client base, as a handy man, were generally much older and hated the computer. They loved him, loved his work and wanted to help him grow, even though they agreed to leave a review, no one did. This is a solution for Scott to get handwritten testimonials, scan the images, attached the images to his website along with some special code so the search engines count those reviews. When done properly, these reviews have significant impact.

Rich Snippets for Local Search

Reviews and testimonials don't have to be on a review site. They can be on your own website.

When review information is marked up in the body of a web page, a search engine can identify it and use it to understand and present the information on your places pages. For example, it can be used to create rich snippets to be displayed on a search results page, or on a Place Page. Review information such as ratings and descriptions can help users to better identify pages with good content.

Beyond improving the presentation of your pages in search results, rich snippets also help users find your website when it references a local place. By using structured markup HTML to describe a business or organization mentioned on your page, you not only improve the Web by making it easier to recognize references to specific places but also help the search engines surface your site in local search results.

Use structured markup to help search engines identify the places mentioned on your site. If your site contains reviews or other information about businesses and organizations, then the structured markup helps precisely correlate your pages with the place mentioned.

With structured markup, such as Microdata or RDF, you can label each piece of text to make it clear that it represents a certain type of data like a business name, an address, or a review rating. This is done by adding HTML tags that help computers understand the data. These tags don't affect the appearance of your pages, but Google and any other services that look at the HTML can use the tags for a more precise understanding of the items referenced on the page.

Review Ratings

Most ratings systems use a 5-point scale

By default, Google assumes that your site uses a 5-point scale, where 5 is the best possible rating and 1 is the worst.

Many reviews sites show ratings on a different scale-for example a rating that ranges from 1-10 points or from 0-100%.

Buyers who complete a Google Checkout transaction will receive an email asking them to review their experience. This doesn't apply for most business, but interesting they are promoting solicitation of reviews, where Yelp is hard against soliciting reviews. I don't promote review solicitation, unless the customer has already verbally expressed a positive experience, in which time you can ask to have those words 'digitized'.

Buyers reviews include a star rating on a scale of one-to-five as well as an optional comment field to discuss delivery time, their customer service experience, and overall satisfaction.

With the introduction of the open social graph at F8 by Facebook, I suspect soon we'll see and open business graph, and using Facebook's comment fields, it's likely and possible we'll see the rating system imposed on their status fields.

Your overall rating score is the average number of stars awarded by all buyers who have posted ratings for you.

Response

If you're unhappy with a buyer's comments, search engines encourage you to contact the buyer directly to resolve any disputes or issues that may have led to a low rating. This is discussed under the topic "Online Reputation Management'.

You may also respond to a review by clicking **Respond publicly** below the buyer's review, which will append your comments on the Review Detail. You can use this field to explain a situation that may have led to the low rating. For example, if the business was closed due to bad weather, you could respond publicly with the note with that reason. The buyer will then have one more opportunity to respond to your statement. These comments will appear beneath your response.

Crawling & Coding

As mentioned, with structured markup you can label each piece of text to make it clear that it represents a certain type of data. This is done by adding HTML tags that help computers understand the data.

You can mark up either individual reviews or aggregate review information—for example, the average rating for a local business or the total number of user reviews submitted.

Review Properties

Google recognizes the following Review properties, derived from the hReview microformat. In general, you can use the same property name for microdata, microformats, and RDFa;

where the microdata/RDFa and microformats property names differ.

Here is the HTML code marked up with microdata:

```
<div>
  <div itemscope itemtype="http://data-
vocabulary.org/Review">
    <span
itemprop="itemreviewed">NAPAREX</span>
    Reviewed by <span
itemprop="reviewer">Ronco</span> on
    <time itemprop="dtreviewed" datetime="2009-
01-06">Jan 6</time>.
    <span itemprop="summary">We Recommend
Naparex!</span>
    <span itemprop="description">I work for an
international telecommunictons company and
NAPAREX has proven time and time again to make
sure all of our shipping needs are taken care
of.  In the face paced industry that we in, it
is imperative that our shipments get to their
destination on time and NAAPREX has always
stuck to their delivery dates.</span>
    Rating: <span itemprop="rating">5</span>
  </div>
</div>
```

There is something I want you to notice here. According to the recommendations, **we're not linking to the user's profiles**.

Add the following code to the markup that links their name to their professional profile.

```
<a href=http://ca.linkedin.com/pub/franco-
raso/6/423/13b>Ronco</a> so it
```

looks like this now

```
<div>
```

```
<div itemscope itemtype="http://data-
vocabulary.org/Review">
    <span
itemprop="itemreviewed">NAPAREX</span>
    Reviewed by <span itemprop="reviewer"><a
href=http://ca.linkedin.com/pub/franco-
raso/6/423/13b>Ronco</a> </span> on
    <time itemprop="dtreviewed" datetime="2009-
01-06">Jan 6</time>.
    <span itemprop="summary">We Recommend
Naparex!</span>
    <span itemprop="description">I work for an
international telecommunictons company and
NAPAREX has proven time and time again to make
sure all of our shipping needs are taken care
of.  In the face paced industry that we in, it
is imperative that our shipments get to their
destination on time and NAAPREX has always
stuck to their delivery dates.</span>
    Rating: <span itemprop="rating">5</span>
  </div>
</div>
```

Once you link to their profile, if the customer is willing, this is the BIG kahuna for trust. Ask them to spread the word of their testimonial on their social media profiles. This closes the link and will assign significant trust to the review directly on the website and will show high in the SERPs.

Local Review Acquisition Strategies

Sometimes you just to do something in life that isn't that much work but has a major impact. This is my review acquisition strategy.

Testimonials and reviews are very important for a variety of different reasons. This is a system that is intended to be implemented into any small business to continually encourage reviews. Motivational systems can also be added to the system to further motivate employees and partners that help encourage reviews. I have no problem giving hundred dollar bonus on a monthly basis to employees who get the most reviews, even for our customers.

I have developed a review acquisition strategy that you can drop into your client's business to help acquire several reviews from reviewers that have high authority.

This is a document that our agency gives to every one of our search marketing customers. Our goal is to give them the education that they need and the management tools in order to continually encourage reviews on their business. They should not solicit reviews ever, but recognize when a customer says something nice about their business that they encourage the customer to make the effort to digitize their complements and leave a review online.

This education is accomplished with this document. In a document provides education on an

- overview of reviews
- what are reviews
- the value of receiving reviews in the online marketing game
- different review sites
- implications to the search engines
- good versus bad reviews and finally
- customer e-mail template for encouraging customer reviews.

The challenge here is that you are relying on your customer to encourage activity inside of their business that demonstrates results that you are measured on. You obviously cannot force your customer to do anything and they are paying you for results. This is where you have to over deliver.

The education in this document provides supportive evidence that reviews are extremely important for their business without the implications of ranking in the search engines. In other words, if the search engines didn't exist this document would still exist.

We provide a little bit of education on conversion and how reviews with a positive rating have increased customer spend by over 20%, provided by a leading web research organization, Comscore.

We also provide some education that your customers will get ahead of the game by establishing trust towards their service area.

Sometimes customers get a little bit scared or concerned about negative reviews online. The fact is that no matter what anybody does they are eventually going to get negative reviews. By introducing the concept of Online Reputation Management, which is another section and topic included in this course, we introduce a new service to the customer and the importance of having the systems in place to measure their online reputation.

We also discussed the importance of and sending your employees and contractors to encourage these reviews. A delivery service person may want to keep their business card with them to hand out to happy customers. The more they hand out the greater their reward.

If a customer ever tells you how much they value your service or asks what they can do for you, ask them for a testimonial. In fact, even if they don't, ask anyway if they've said they like your service! Testimonials are *that* valuable.

Local Review Sites

A review site is a <u>website</u> where reviews can be posted about businesses, products, or services. In some cases, even people. These days, these websites are using <u>Web 2.0</u> techniques to gather reviews from customers. Sometimes they may employ professional writers to author reviews on the topic of concern for the site.

Review sites are typically also portal sites and data aggregators. However, not all review sites are portal site and not all portal sites are review sites. For this reason we have to classify certain sites as review sites.

Industry Perception

Many, in fact most review sites make little attempt to control postings, or to verify the reviews. Faultfinders claim that positive reviews are sometimes written by the businesses or individuals being reviewed, while negative reviews might be written by competitors, disgruntled employees, or anyone with a grudge against the business being reviewed. In addition, studies of research methodology have shown that in forums where people are able to post opinions publicly, group polarization often occurs, and the result is very positive comments, very negative comments, and little in between, meaning that those who would have been in the middle are either silent or pulled to one extreme or the other. This is critical to understand. As you implement a review acquisition strategy for your customers it is imperative that you identify and focus on your clients top customers immediately to leave reviews. This will initially establish a positive should group polarization occur in your clients profile page. Another criticism against sites that rely on income from businesses is that they are reluctant to post negative since that undermines their business model. This leads to a conflict of interest.

The fact is that the review sites, like Google, want to filter all the garbage. Sometimes they don't get it right, but they are always looking to improve their algorithms. We have to assume they are getting better daily, like Google with their algorithm for search. With this assumption it makes no sense to me to game the review filters. It's like chasing the algorithm. We shouldn't be focusing on either quantity or quality of reviews, but focus on the natural organic adoption or reviews with existing customers. I feel if this is our objective we will always meet the needs set forth by the review sites.

Forget those Critics!

Most review sites admit that reviews may not be objective, and that ratings may not be statistically valid. I know this will work itself out over time. Most consumers are yet trained to leave reviews. Many businesses have yet adopted a acquisition strategy. If the trends continue, like a 100% increase in reviews for Yelp in 2010, then this is likely the year that'll curb much of this critics. It's for this reason that we tested profile review authority and sure enough, different profiles are assigned different levels of trust. Just focus on quality and you'll clear those filters. Let's talk more about filters now.

Review Filters

As we have been talking about all of the review sites have review filters. Here's some information about those filters.

Reviews that reflect perfectly legitimate experiences are sometimes filtered out by the review filter's algorithmic processes. Don't worry about this. To solve this, have the reviewer leave additional, unbiased reviews for other local businesses. Within a few weeks, that reviewers profile filter should be lifted.

Reviews are never deleted by the review filter; they are always shown on users' profile pages but not the business that is being reviewed unless you dig deep. The review filter simply groups established users' reviews from their user pages onto business pages. This automated process sometimes creates the perception that reviews are being deleted and re-added over time; what's actually happening is users are becoming more-or-less established over time.

The best word of mouth is organic and unsolicited. As counter-intuitive as it may seem, Yelp discourages business owners from asking people to write reviews about their businesses. It's tough for an algorithm to tell the difference between a business owner aggressively putting a laptop in front of a client and saying, "Give me 5 stars!" and that same business owner flipping the laptop around and manufacturing a fake 5-star review about themselves. Follow my review acquisition process to avoid violating the T & C's of Yelp and others, yet still have the systems to drive unsolicited, organic reviews.

Both positive and negative reviews can be affected. This is to protect Dentist A from Dentist B's writing of malicious 1-star reviews about his competitor.

SEO helps here too. Identifying relevant, authoritative sites to have links going to a user's profile will increase the trust and authority for that profile, as long as it's relevant sites and not just link building.

Local Reviews Website List

This should not be confused as the data provider list to acquire citations. The list is very similar, but these reviews sites are listed in order of review preference. Please be aware as these companies grow and change, some might be better, others might get worse. Use this list priority with a grain of salt and do your due diligence to uncover other sites.

- Google
- Yelp
- City Search
- Yahoo Local
- InsiderPages
- Angie's List
- Judy's Book
- Superpages
- Merchant Circle
- Insider Pages

Top Ten Strategies for Local Rankings

This is a comprehensive list of the top ten items of completion for a local business to rank #1 in the search engines. Now that you have gained a fundamental knowledge of what Internet Marketing is for you and what it means for your business, this list can follow as your action plan.

Follow this link on your computer or scan the QR code to view this on the Internet and get additional tools to help you plan and execute.

http://www.scott-gallagher.net/top-10-local-seo-strategies

Get your own QR code for your business at http://www.localmarketingsource.com/qr-code-generator/

1. Profiles

Establishing your profiles' authority is critical. Follow Google's Best Practices Guide, which can be found by googling "Google Best Practice Guide".

You will need to claim your listings, as chances are your business is already listed. While there's a long list of places to profile your business, you really need to claim at least Google, Bing, Yahoo and Superpages before moving onto the next step.

Follow the bullet points below to create profiles that have authority.

- Verify and Claim your Listings at http://www.getlisted.org
    - Claim at least Google, Bing, Yahoo and Superpages
- Complete all info thoroughly, including clear, long, excellent description (Basic and Enhanced Information)
- Establish NAP format
- Use email matching domain to register account
- Establish photo shoots with Google when possible. Always upload at least 5 pictures or more.
- Use images and video, (walk-through, testimonials) as much as possible!
- Establish Service area
- Utilize QR Codes when possible
- Real Address, No UPS or PO Boxes
- Consider implications of Walk-in versus Service Based

Stay Away from:

- Violating Google's Terms and Conditions

- Using 800 Numbers
- Using Phone Number Tracking
- P.O. / UPS Boxes
- Multiple Place Pages / location
- Duplicate Phone on Multiple Place Pages

2. Reviews

Implement a Review Acquisition System. We do this for all of our clients.

As previously discussed, it's a violation to solicit reviews. Our Review Acquisition System does not solicit reviews, we simply implement the systems and procedures in the business to have a lending hear for quality compliments. In turn, we make it simple to digitally capture that compliment, making it a review.

For a copy of the LMS Review Acquisition Strategy we implement with our clients, follow this URL or use your smart phone to scan the QR code.

http://bit.ly/review_acquisition

- Professional Service offices should create a 'Thank You' post card when a thank you mentioned in the office, including instructions to leave a review on Zagat.
- Properly train employees to have a lending ear for positive feedback from customers, patients and clients.
- Encourage positive customers to leave a review online.
- Use the hReview HTML Rich Snippet Markup on Website for reviews.
  - o Link Reviewers' name to their online social profile, preferably LinkedIn.

- Do not solicit reviews. Only ask to leave a digital review if a verbal unsolicited testimonial is provided.

3. Social Media

Create and participate in social media channels

    I.   Create a Business Page or Fan Page
- i. Facebook (Get Vanity URL after 25 likes)
- ii. Google+ Local
- iii. LinkedIn

    II.   Follow Best Practices
- i. Photos
- ii. Descriptions
- iii. Links
- iv. Product / Services
- v. SEO Optimization

    III.   Engage with Audience
- i. Add value
- ii. Use LinkedIn for B2B Sales
- iii. Online Reputation Management Strategy

4. Citations

Citations are web references. Consider your business, your industry, your locality. There are a variety of websites that participate in those communities. Where have you frequenting public locations for new business? Such as the Chamber of Commerce. You can have citation on many types of sites, but your BEST citation if your own website.

Make sure you follow consistent formatting for your NAP.

Acquire citations from as many of the following sources.

Public Sources

- Annual Reports, SEC Information

- Federal, State and City Gov'ts
- Business Magazines
- Newspapers
- Postal Service Information

Data Providers & Review Sites

- Superpages
- infoUSA
- Theme Sites
- Yelp
- Citysearch
- InsiderPages
- Google
- Yahoo Local
- Angie's List
- Judy's Book

Outside the Box

- ATM or Kiosk at your location? List in directories
- National Register of Historic Places
- Free Wifi Directories (if you have wifi in your office)
- RedBox Directory
- Sponsorships / Charity Events
- Speaking Engagements
- Host a Weather Station

5. Video

Local Businesses can create and distribute at least four types of video. Video is very easy to create, even with an iPhone. Here are four simple types of video that can be created for most business types.

I. Office / Warehouse Walkthrough
II. Testimonial Video
III. Operational (for product / service)
IV. Commercial (advertisement for product / service)

- Distribution to YouTube is critical. Optimize video title and description. Clear concise title that is keyword rich. Include link in description.
- Promote through Social Channels once distributed and optimized.

6. Local PR

Create and distribute an effective press release. Hire a local writer from the local news paper. Distribute the local press release to at least ten local publications, including:

- Local Newspaper
- Regional Newspaper
- Local FREE Publications (pick one up a Chiropractor's office)
- Local Chamber of Commerce
- Local College – Approach business admin

Try to have at least one new press release that is news worthy for your business once every quarter.

7. Website On-The-Page SEO

This is only a partial list of the factors and represents the most important items to complete on your website. You can give these instructions to your web developer. Remember, this really only helps the search engines fully understand what your website is all about and giving it credibility. This will not improve conversion on your website.

1. Validate your HTML code so it is "spider" compliant. http://validator.w3.org/
2. Text link navigation at the bottom of the page. Use your keywords as anchor text.
3. The Title Tag should be compelling and keyword focused.
4. Your description tag needs to work hand-in-hand with the Title to get the searcher to "click" on the listing.
5. Every page should have a unique (60% of the words completely original) Title & Description.
6. H1 tag should be used and should be very compelling
7. Add ALT tags to your main graphics and do not attempt to fool the Search Engines here.
8. Place your keyword phrase in the following areas:
   i. Title Tag
   ii. Meta Description
   iii. H1 tag to begin the content
   iv. First paragraph of content
   v. Appearing in Bold or Italic in the first three paragraphs of content (if possible, not that big of a deal)
   vi. Appearing in the filename (or directory name)
   vii. Used in anchor text to either an internal page or relevant external site.
9. Fix bad links and create XML Sitemap and submit to Google.

8. Company Blog

This is a critical piece for any Internet Marketing Strategy for a business. Almost every piece of marketing communication can be hosted on a blog including all types of media. Try to get a new blog post once a week. Here are some tips on for your blog.

- Use WordPress Self Hosted. It's free, hosting is cheap.
- Use SEO Plugins (Yoast is my favorite)
- Blog Weekly
- Internal Links to your Website on blog posts
- Opt-in Conversion Optimization (Welcome Gate / PopUp / Scipt). Consider an email auto responder once they opt-in.
- Create compelling content prospects can relate to

9. External Links

Link Building is critical for Organic SEO Rankings in the SERPs. Find sources to link to the following pages, including your root domain. Remember, links are not citations. You can have a link from another blog to your website, or an industry forum. There is a lengthy strategy behind links, but for the purpose of ranking a business, building links is your last major activity you should be working on. If everything else is done properly, links will come organically...which is essence is ironic since links are the premise for original organic ranking.

Location Based Pages

- Local newspaper (PR Campaigns)
- Chamber or Networking Groups
- J.V's
- Local Directories / Phonebooks

Theme Related Pages

- Directories / Data Providers
- Social Networking Groups and Sites
- High Authority Exposure

10. Systems for Measurement and Correction

Create the systems for measurement in your business, and measure at least the following items for your online marketing campaign.

Bob Parsons, CEO of GoDaddy said "Everything that is measured, improves".

Here are some resources and tips on what to measure.

I.   Claimed Listings (you can use getlisted.org or download this worksheet we use at http://bit.ly/asset_inventory)
II. Keyword Rankings (We use a company called Bright Local to automate our rankings)
III. KW Strategy (evaluate your KW strategy regularly and post list to review regularly)
IV. Competitive Research
V.   Citation Acquisition Strategy (we use the following worksheet as a basis to monitor our citation strategy http://bit.ly/asset_inventory)

What to do now

Thank you for reading this far. Chances are you have some interest in Local Internet Marketing. Perhaps you own your own local business, or you work for one, perhaps you'd like to offer this service to companies in your area. I begun by offering this service to a specific industry in 2005, the Courier industry.

Regardless, you are now in a position that you need to take some action. You may feel like you do not know enough to dive into this yourself right now, but if that is the position you are in, pretty much taking action on any of the strategies discussed will help you. Just follow the Top Ten Strategy.

Truth is most business owners and managers already have enough on their plate and are required to hire someone. First, please speak with at least three different companies. They don't mind providing proposals. Most firms will provide you with a free analysis of your situation and explain what they need to do to get your results.

Don't accept guarantees on results. Expect intended results, benched against their previous client results. Understand how long it's expected to take to get expected results, and ensure they let you know everything they are doing to get those results.

Today I operate my marketing agency in Algonquin, IL named WON Marketing Inc. We service local businesses, with a focus on the Chiropractic industry and we still hold roots in the transportation industry.

I would like to an opportunity to earn your business.

My company will provide you with a free full online analysis of your company. At the end of this book you'll find what we'll do for you. We understand we might not be a fit for you, but on the other hand, if we can offer value and a return on your investment with confidence, our relationship could be very mutually benefiting. Visit www.WONMarketing.com to learn more.

Learn how to Build and Manage an Agency

With over 23 million local small businesses in the United States, there is much opportunity for several quality-marketing firms. Since this is a geographically sound business, understanding local culture is critical, leaving opportunity.

I teach this practice through a variety of avenues including an extensive on-demand video portal, private Facebook group, weekly member calls and regular updated content. Our material extends to several agency principals and includes our popular SEO Sales Trail, all the tools you needs to acquire valuable new business.

We provide several free training resources and useful tools for free. Check us out, you can learn more about our affordable membership at Local Marketing Source, LLC.

Visit www.localmarketingsource.com or scan the following QR code.

WON Marketing Online Analysis

This is what we'll do for you, for free! You can then chose to give this education and these FREE reports to your current team, your secretary or hire us! Here's what you get.

Driving Qualified Traffic

- Keyword Research for your top 5 revenue converting keywords.
- Onsite Website Report on your website to what is wrong with the site from the eyes of the Search Engines.
- Competitive Analysis Report on why competitors outrank you in Google and who's strategy needs to be evaluated.
- Specific steps to create the right mix of online exposure so you can rank high. If implemented, results could yield front page results, providing more leads.

Converting Traffic

- Audience Group Analysis, delivering the right message to the right audience groups
- Identify the objective and minimum objective of each audience group
- Tips and Suggestions to improve conversion of each group
- A System to immediately implement to properly measure all of your Internet Marketing success. Everything measured Improves.

Set up your personalized analysis now. We want the opportunity to prove to you we know what we are doing, we provide a service that will get you #1 in your area and we are very well priced.

Visit http://bit.ly/wm_analysis or scan the QR code to learn more about your free comprehensive analysis for your business with WON Marketing.

www.ingramcontent.com/pod-product-compliance
Lightning Source LLC
Chambersburg PA
CBHW060404190526
45169CB00002B/738